T0208220

After You Have Suffered a While . . .

A Book for Abused Women

Robbie Cox-White

WESTBOW
PRESS®
A DIVISION OF THOMAS NELSON
& ZONDERVAN

Copyright © 2019 Robbie Cox-White.

All rights reserved. No part of this book may be used or reproduced by any means, graphic, electronic, or mechanical, including photocopying, recording, taping or by any information storage retrieval system without the written permission of the author except in the case of brief quotations embodied in critical articles and reviews.

Scripture taken from the King James Version of the Bible.

This book is a work of non-fiction. Unless otherwise noted, the author and the publisher make no explicit guarantees as to the accuracy of the information contained in this book and in some cases, names of people and places have been altered to protect their privacy.

WestBow Press books may be ordered through booksellers or by contacting:

WestBow Press
A Division of Thomas Nelson & Zondervan
1663 Liberty Drive
Bloomington, IN 47403
www.westbowpress.com
1 (866) 928-1240

Because of the dynamic nature of the Internet, any web addresses or links contained in this book may have changed since publication and may no longer be valid. The views expressed in this work are solely those of the author and do not necessarily reflect the views of the publisher, and the publisher hereby disclaims any responsibility for them.

Any people depicted in stock imagery provided by Getty Images are models, and such images are being used for illustrative purposes only.
Certain stock imagery © Getty Images.

ISBN: 978-1-9736-5999-0 (sc)
ISBN: 978-1-9736-6000-2 (e)

Print information available on the last page.

WestBow Press rev. date: 5/8/2019

Contents

"Out of suffering have emerged the strongest souls; the most massive characters are seared with scars."

Khalil Gibran

The Plan Of Salvation

The following Scriptures will show you the plan that Jesus Christ has for your life. This plan will show you that you are a sinner and need to accept Jesus Christ in your life as your personal Savior.

1. We are all sinners. Romans 3:23
   "For all have sinned and come short of the glory of God;"
2. There is a price or a penalty for sin. Romans 6:23 *"For the wages of sin is death, but the gift of God is eternal life through Jesus Christ our Lord".*
3. God's love for sinners. Romans 5:8
   "But God commendeth His love toward us, in that, while we were yet sinners, Christ died for us."
4. You must believe and confess. Romans 10:9
   "That if thou shalt confess with thy mouth the Lord Jesus, and shalt believe in thine heart that God hath raised Him from the dead, thou shalt be saved".

If you will do what God has asked you to do in these Scriptures and ask Jesus Christ to come into your heart, you will be saved. You will be saved from your sins and have an eternal home in Heaven. He is waiting to be your Savior. Just pray and ask Him into your heart.

Dedication

This book "After You Have Suffered A While…" is dedicated to women who have been victims of any type of abuse. The type of abuse may be rape, physical abuse, sexual abuse/molestation, or any other type of violent act. The woman may have been a victim of a crime such as a robbery or a mugging. Maybe she has been a victim of stalking. There is also verbal and emotional abuse. This book was written to reach out to the countless number of women who have been "Suffering in Silence".

RCW

Acknowledgements and Thanks

A Very Special thanks to all those who supported me during the process of writing this book:

First, to my Dad, Mr. John Robert Cox- you are the best, as always.

Then, to my son and daughter-in-law, Jordan and Maddie White, thanks for all the love and encouragement.

To my sister-in-law, Carolyn Massey, for your love, and always listening when I needed an ear.

To my pastors, Brother Jacob Gray and Brother Ben Jones, thank you for your prayers and encouragement, as well.

To my best friend, Sandy Kehrer, for having confidence in me when I had none in myself.

Thanks to my counselor and Sister-in-Christ, Teresa Miller, who always believed in me.

Words cannot express the overwhelming amount of gratitude I feel to those that donated money to help publish this book. Thank you for having faith in me and believing in my cause. May God richly reward each and every one.

A heartfelt thanks to the folks at Westbow Publishing Company. You walked me through each phase of the publishing process with much kindness and graciousness. I wouldn't have made it without your guidance and direction.

Finally, and certainly not least, a very large shout-out to Mr. Gabe Martin, PA-C. Gabe has walked this journey of life with me as my therapist and counselor. He has taught me the skills I have. He has been my "go-to" each step of the way. He demonstrated the compassion of Christ along with true professionalism. Together, we will carry on the mission of this book.

May God richly bless each and every one!

Of course, thanks to my Heavenly Father, the Author of all authors who wrote the Book of the Ages, the Bible. He gave me the vision to write the book. He is the true Author of this book. May He alone be glorified!

RCW

Anna the Prophetess: An Introduction

Anna the Prophetess was a Jewish woman who lived during the time of the Messiah's birth. She was of a great age and had been a widow for 84 years. She was a Prophetess that lived in one of the temple apartments. According to the Scriptures, she "served God with fastings and prayers night and day". Luke 2:37. Mary and Joseph brought the baby Jesus to the temple when He was eight days old, according to Jewish custom and the Jewish law. When Anna came in the temple, she immediately knew He was the Messiah. She instantly began to give thanks unto the Lord. When Jewish people came to the temple, looking for the Messiah, she told them about Jesus. Anna the Prophetess was the first woman to lay eyes on the Messiah except for His mother, Mary.

Dake's Annotated Reference Bible has this commentary on Anna:

"As many women represented their sex in all historic events in Scripture, so Anna here represents women in the greatest of all events – the revelation of Messiah."

Anna the Prophetess is only mentioned in the Scriptures in this one passage, but she is held in highest honor among historians. She dedicated her life to the service of God. Her reward was absolutely beautiful- to be the first woman to lay eyes on the baby Messiah, except for his mother, Mary. How fulfilling that must have been for her. At a great old age, and widowed for 84 years, to have the opportunity to see baby Jesus, and then proclaim to others that the Messiah had arrived. How precious!

RCW

Preface

The book of Luke, chapter 2, verses 36-38, introduces us to a very famous widow. Her name was Anna and she was a Prophetess. According to Scripture, she was an elderly widow who devoted her life to the service of the Lord. She lived in the temple and served the Lord with prayers and fasting. As an honor to Anna, I have begun a ministry called "Anna's Healing Ministries". This book is a part of the outreach of the new ministries.

This inspirational book has been written and designed to address emotional needs of women who have been traumatized. Oftentimes, these women have been "Suffering in Silence" for many years. There may be different reasons. Maybe they were too ashamed to admit they had a need; or no one understood their needs; or no one was listening to their cries. The women have been traumatized as a result of different types of abuse. Some of the types of abuse include sexual or physical assault, rape, domestic violence, battered women's syndrome, Post-Traumatic Stress Disorder, homelessness and/ or neglect.

I am a widow, like Anna. I have also devoted my life to God's service. I have experienced many types of traumatic episodes. In this book you will find the various types of abuse I experienced. Most of the time, no one knew I was suffering. However, my emotions were completely out of control. I have addressed how each of the different topics affected me. Sometimes, the situations were unique to each other; other times, they overlapped. The only way I could find comfort during any of these storms was to cry out to God and turn to His Holy Scriptures for comfort. In this book, you will find some of my favorite Scriptures that gave me comfort during my distress. My prayer is that as you read these pages, the Holy Spirit will minister emotional healing and comfort, as only He can. This book is not my book. It belongs to my Heavenly Father. May you receive warmth and comfort in your soul.

May He use it to heal your wounds and draw you closer to Him is my prayer.

RCW

"But the God of all grace, who hath called us unto His eternal glory by Christ Jesus, after that ye have suffered a while, make you perfect, stablish, strengthen, settle you."

1 Peter 5:10(KJV)

Childhood

During my childhood, I lived with my parents and older sister in a small town. Located in Southern Illinois, we lived a quiet life. My Dad worked in the oil-fields and Mom was a stay-at-home Mom. They were honest, God-fearing people who took us church every time the doors were open. I always tell everyone I had a drug problem. I was "drug" to church. My Grandfather Cox was an old-fashioned Pentecostal preacher. He would actually walk the railroad tracks to small country churches just to preach the gospel. The churches would always take an offering for him, but he would put the money back in the offering plate. He didn't want to be accused of being "greedy of filthy lucre." (Scripture reference I Timothy 3:3).

My sister and I were both very good students in school. My sister graduated as Valedictorian of her class. I was in fifth place in my class. The school librarian would allow both of us to assist her in the library. I have always loved to read. I have been known to read a book more than once, if the book is an exceptional read.

So, as you can see, I have a blend of faith and education in my background. Around 1963-1964, between ages 6 and 7, I began to feel the guilt, shame and condemnation associated with the sin that was in my life. I realized I was a sinner even though I had been brought up in Sunday school and church.

Just As I Am

"Just as I am, without one plea,

But that Thy blood was shed for me,

And that Thou biddest me come to Thee,

O Lamb of God, I come! I come!"

Robbie Cox-White

As they would sing this beautiful hymn at church, I began to realize my need of Jesus as my Savior. Even at that young age, the Holy Ghost was drawing me to Christ. Since I was so young, I wasn't sure what I was supposed to do. But yet, I knew God was dealing with my heart. At the same time, I just continued going to school and learning as much as I could.

Guilt

Guilt is a negative emotion which is experienced by almost all women. Guilt is a very strong emotion I deal with on a very personal level. I have a tendency to blame myself when something has gone wrong, even though I may not have had anything to do with the situation. I am constantly saying, "I'm sorry", even though I had nothing to be sorry about. It seems as though a lot of women are like that. Women are made to feel responsible for so many different things. When something goes wrong, it is automatically our fault, right? We are taught to feel like this, but it is part of our upbringing. We cannot be made to feel guilty over everything that goes wrong. At the same time, we cannot make everyone happy all of the time.

When a woman is victimized or abused, guilt is one of the first things she hears inside her mind. She thinks it had to be her fault. She knows beyond the shadow of a doubt that she did something to cause the abuse to happen. Or, maybe there was something she could have done to stop it from happening; or maybe she just thinks she said the wrong thing. Whatever thoughts are running through her mind, there's a pretty good chance that she is automatically blaming herself. She is torturing herself inside her mind trying to figure out where she went wrong. Abuse victims are somehow programmed to think like that. But that type of thinking is totally wrong. A victim of abuse or trauma is exactly that- a victim. She should be treated like a victim. She should be given all the support she needs, and the reassurance that she has done nothing wrong.

There is one area in our lives where we are all guilty, however. We are all born sinners, which automatically makes us guilty of sin. The cause of this goes back to Adam and Eve in the Garden of Eden. Adam and Eve lied to God and, as a result, cursed all of mankind. We are all guilty of sin from birth. Romans 3:23 states, "*for all have sinned and come short of the glory of God*".

But that doesn't mean we are without hope. God is merciful and just. He has provided a way for us to be delivered from our sinful nature and become one of His children. All you have to do is admit that you are a sinner, and that Christ died on the cross of Calvary for the sins of mankind. Then you must believe in your heart that Jesus is Lord. You must confess

3

with your mouth that He lives in your heart. If you will do these things, you will become saved. All your sins have been covered by the blood of Jesus. There is no more reason to feel guilty. You are a child of God and everything from your past has been cleansed. All of your sins-past, present, and future are covered by the blood of Christ. When Jesus sets you free, you are free indeed. The apostle Paul states in the book of Galatians, chapter 5:1,

"Stand fast therefore in the liberty wherewith Christ hath made us free and be not entangled again with the yoke of bondage."

He gives you sweet victory. There is an old song called "Victory in Jesus". Here's how it goes:

Chorus

"Oh, victory in Jesus,

My Savior forever,

He sought me and bought me

With His redeeming blood;

He loved me 'ere I knew Him, and all my love is due Him.

He plunged me to victory beneath the cleansing flood."

In 1965, I was eight years old. I was at church one Sunday night. It was the last night of our Vacation Bible School, called the Evangelistic service. The minister gave the invitation. The first song they sang was, "Jesus, Hold My Hand". They began to softly play the beautiful hymn, "The Old Rugged Cross." I had known for a long time that the Holy Ghost had been dealing with my heart to accept Christ as my personal Savior. I went to the altar that night and gave my heart to the Lord.

That was over fifty years ago. He set me free that night from my chains of sin and bondage. He will do the same for you, if you will repent of your sins and ask Him to be the Lord of your life. He will remove the guilt of sin when you trust Him to be your Savior. He will also take the false guilt associated with the episode of abuse from your mind. You will have no need to carry that baggage around with you. It is false guilt, because you did absolutely nothing to cause the abuse to happen. It is not your fault. You did not ask to be abused. You can turn those feelings over to Jesus, and He will take them away. Find someone to talk to about those feelings. Share them with someone else. Do not keep them bottled inside. Stop "Suffering in Silence".

Shame

Oftentimes, as a little girl, my mother would scold me. She would say "aren't you ashamed of yourself", or" I would be ashamed if I were you." She was a perfectionist and didn't realize the amount of pressure she was putting on me. Then, of course, I never felt like anything I did quite measured up. So, I constantly felt ashamed of anything I ever did. If something bad did happen, like a friendship or relationship failed, her immediate response was, "Well, it's no wonder. The way you act around people, I'd be ashamed!"; or, "you know it's your fault. I tried to tell you, but you wouldn't listen". I constantly felt ashamed and questioned myself as to why I couldn't do better, or, even why I wasn't a better person.

Oftentimes, after a woman has been traumatized, she feels a tremendous amount of shame. The shame can and does come from many sources. If she was a victim of domestic violence, her husband will more than likely make her feel ashamed because she wasn't a better wife. Or if she was a victim of battered wife's syndrome, she was blamed and shamed because she didn't do something exactly right. If she was a rape victim, the rape was automatically her fault because she was "asking for it" or dressed inappropriately. The shame associated with victims of child molestation is absolutely indescribable. The offender, law enforcement, attorneys, judges, and others in authority will oftentimes add to the victim's feelings of shame. Sometimes, even her family and so-called friends make her feel ashamed. Then, of course, there is the shame she is putting on herself in her own mind.

It took me a long time to get over those feelings of shame. Since they mostly came from my mother, they were so deep inside of me, they were actually a part of who I was. But then, I began to study God's Word. I found several Scriptures that address deliverance from shame. Psalms 25:2 deals with trusting in God,

"O my God I trust in Thee: let me not be ashamed, let not mine enemies triumph over me."

In Romans 5:5, the apostle Paul states,

"And hope maketh not ashamed; because the love of God is shed abroad in our hearts by the Holy Ghost which is given unto us".

Romans 10:11 states,

"...*for the scripture saith, Whosoever believeth on Him shall not be ashamed*".

The secret of deliverance from shame is to know the truth which sets us free. John 8:32 states,

"*And ye shall know the truth and the truth shall make you free*";

and John 8:36 states," *If the Son therefore shall make you free, ye shall be free indeed.*"

I Surrender All

The root word for condemnation is condemn, which means to be judged. I cannot begin to count the times I have been judged by someone who had no idea what they were talking about. After I had been through a gut-wrenching experience, the last thing I needed was someone who had no idea what I went through making judgements about me. But that was what happened. That made me even more reluctant to come forward and tell anyone about my traumatic event. Yes, I was traumatized, and I was "Suffering in Silence" It was years before I was able to talk about certain things. When I finally accepted God's love and grace in the fullness, I began to see things differently.

More often than not, when a woman is a victim of abuse, she is judged harshly. People can't seem to realize she has been abused. So, rather than believe her and be supportive, they automatically doubt her word. She is called a liar, someone who is seeking attention, or even mentally ill. A lot of the times, the judgement is coming from the professionals who are supposed to be helping her find the guilty party. But a woman does not have to be a victim of abuse to be judged by others. Sometimes, they are judged by whether they are rich or poor; by the type of car they drive; by their weight; by their level of education, just to name a few things. No one has the right to judge anyone. Judgements pierce the soul and can cause more damage than one can possibly realize. Sometimes, the damage can last a lifetime and the person can never seem to rise above it.

Once we become believers, if we are walking in God's truth, there is no reason to feel condemnation any longer. The blood of Jesus Christ cleanses us from all unrighteousness; however, sometimes, we still struggle with those feelings. After a lifetime of harsh criticism and judgement, it is hard to understand we are loved by Jesus. God's grace is always available to help us work through those negative feelings and accept ourselves as who we are in Christ. The apostle Paul gives us a Scripture in Romans 8:1 to help us overcome condemnation.

"There is therefore now no condemnation to them which are in Christ Jesus, who walk not after the flesh, but after the Spirit".

All we need to do as believers in Christ is to pray and surrender all those negative things that have been said about us. Read the Bible and let Him speak to you through His Word.

I Surrender All

"All to Jesus I surrender, All to Him I freely give.

I will ever love and trust Him, In His presence daily live.

Chorus

I surrender all, I surrender all,

All to Thee, my blessed Savior

I surrender all".

At The Cross

This is the chorus of one of the most beloved hymns of all times:

Chorus

"So I'll cherish the old rugged cross,

Where my trophies at last I lay down;

I will cling to the old rugged cross

And exchange it someday for a crown."

The old rugged cross. A precious emblem for the blood-bought of Jesus Christ. Where He hung between two thieves on Calvary's hill. Where every last drop of His precious blood was shed. For our sins. For our salvation. For our healing. For our deliverance. For our cleansing. For our burdens. What a pitiful sight for eyes to behold. The Blessed Savior, King of Kings, stretched across a piece of wood: nails in His hands and His feet; a wounded side; a crown of thorns on His head; stripes on His back; blood and water coming forth from His side. Our Savior, crucified.

But, wait-look a little closer. There are bags under the cross. Lots and lots of bags. They look like money bags. They have elastic at the top with drawstrings. The drawstrings are pulled tightly in a bow and then knotted. Secure. Very secure. Nothing will escape from these bags-absolutely nothing.

And look, look again. There is someone walking to the cross. Very slowly-as if not to disturb anything. Quietly. Reverently to the foot of the cross. Tip-toeing around the tied up, sealed bags. It is me. My arms are loaded down with more bags. Identical bags-securely sealed. There are so many bags. They are so heavy, I can barely carry them. My arms are heavy-laden under the load.

I lay each bag under the foot of the cross, where the Precious Blood flows down. I lovingly gaze at the wounded Lamb of God, with tears flowing down my face. I am reminded of the words to an old song, "Take your burdens to the Lord and leave them there..." I turn and walk away from the cross. But then, I turn around and look back. Each bag has a white label on it. On that label is a name-my name-Robbie Cox-White.

Yes, those bags were filled with burdens. Burdens that belonged to me. Burdens of sin; sickness; disease; depression; guilt; shame; emotional pain, etc. But I placed each burden in a bag. Then I secured the bag so tightly that nothing could escape-absolutely nothing. I placed every full heavy bag at the foot of my Savior's cross. The old rugged cross. Where His blood was shed. Then, after tears of prayer and thanksgiving, I walked away. Free from my burdens. Peace in my heart and mind. Walked away to continue life's journey, singing this old hymn:

"At the cross, at the cross, where I first saw the light

And the burden of my heart rolled away.

It was there by faith I received my sight,

And now I am happy all the day".

Then, I went home and looked up these Scriptures from the Bible:

"*Surely He hath borne our griefs and carried our sorrows: yet did we esteem Him stricken, smitten of God and afflicted. He was wounded for our transgressions, He was bruised for our iniquities: the chastisement of our peace was upon Him and with His stripes we are healed*". Isaiah 53:4-5.

Yes, there is a cross. A cross on which our Savior was crucified. Every drop of His life-giving blood was shed on that cross. The blood that runs down Calvary's mountain. There is power in the blood of Jesus. Power to save lost souls from sin. Power to deliver from every burden. Jesus has already taken care of our burdens. He doesn't want us to carry our burdens. He is our burden-bearer. I made my first trip of many to that cross in 1965. I still go there to give my burdens to my Savior. Even though we may not be able to see through our blinding tears, He has made us a promise that we should never forget:

"*And we know that all things work together for the good to them that love God and are the called according to His purpose*". Romans 8:28.

Amazing Grace

Part 1

This chapter begins with the year 1993. In that year, I met the most wonderful man, named Cary White. He was originally from Georgia and was living in a town about five miles from me in Mt. Vernon, IL. I was divorced; and he, too, was single. A friend introduced us, and it was pretty much love at first sight. We dated for a while, and then we got married. Shortly afterward, I found out I was pregnant with our son, Jordan. We moved to Georgia in 1994, where Cary could find a good job. We struggled, as young couples often do, but we were very happy.

On March 3rd, 2003, I had a heart attack. It came totally out of nowhere; we didn't even know I had heart problems. I was only 45 years old. I was at home on a Saturday night. I was lying on the couch, watching TV. My husband, Cary, wanted to call the ambulance. I kept telling him I would be alright. The pain in my chest continued. It was getting worse, but I still refused to go to the hospital. Finally, our son, Jordan, walked in the living room. He took one look at me and grabbed the phone from his dad. Jordan dialed 911. When the ambulance arrived, my Blood pressure was 220/180. I was immediately taken to the hospital and admitted overnight.

The next morning, around 3:00a.m., I had just a small twinge of chest pain. The nurse called the doctor, who immediately admitted me to the Intensive Care Unit. I did not know I had suffered a heart attack until after I was discharged from the hospital. The doctor told Cary not to tell me how critical I was. The doctor was afraid the news would "scare me to death". Again, I was only 45 years old.

I was recovering from the heart attack when my sister, Karen, called from Michigan. She told me she had been diagnosed with terminal breast cancer. The doctors had given her less than six months to live. She called me on March 31, 2003. She was the picture of health. She was at her ideal weight. She rode her bike five miles a day. She swam five files a day. She had an extremely large garden. She enjoyed every moment of being outdoors that the cold, cruel Michigan weather would permit. She even chopped wood for fuel for their winter heat.

11

All of this, in addition to being a wife and wonderful mother to three lovely girls. There was no way I could comprehend the idea of giving her up in six months! Absolutely not! We talked after she was initially diagnosed. At first, she decided against any type of treatments. Then, her doctors told her how the condition would progress without treatments, so she decided to take chemotherapy.

I was living in Georgia and she was living Michigan. She had three young daughters. I felt so helpless. I asked what I could do to help her. She told me to "keep her laughing". That was in March, 2003. She took treatments and valiantly fought her battle with Stage 4 breast cancer. And she won! I spoke with her on Thanksgiving Day, of 2003, and her cancer was in remission! I remember thinking that she would be around for a long time. I actually remember thinking that she would be around to see my grandchildren grown, and I didn't have any grandchildren.

Four days later, I received a phone call from my dad, who was still living in Illinois. He could barely speak. He said, "She's gone," and was crying. I said, "Oh, no, mom?" And he said, "No, it's Karen. She's gone". I could hardly believe it. I had just spoken with her four days earlier and she was fine. But, now, she was gone. She had suffered a massive heart attack. She had three precious children. When her oldest daughter came home from college one afternoon, she went in the house to take a nap. When she woke up, she realized it was dark, and her mother was not in the house. She went outside to look for her. She found her outside in the yard, where she had been doing yard work, with her favorite dog lying by her side.

Immediately, I began to pack to make the trip to Illinois. Cary, Jordan and I were going to stop in Illinois to pick up my Dad to attend my sister's memorial services in Michigan. My Mother was in the Nursing Home with dementia and was unable to travel. We left Georgia around 10:00 that next morning to go to Dad's. We arrived at Dad's house at about 8:00 that night. The first thing he said was, "Robbie, you are not going to believe what has happened around here. The Nursing Home called and said they had to take your Mother to the hospital. She is in Congestive Heart Failure".

So, I had to choose between life and death. We stayed at Dad's to be with him and Mom. I knew my sister would have it no other way. We missed my sister's memorial services. She passed away on December 2, 2003.

Part 2

Now, let me fast forward to 2005. My Mother passed away on May 10th, 2005. It was on Mother's Day. I was still living in Georgia, with Cary and Jordan. I was talking to her on the phone, and she said she wasn't feeling well, and wanted to lay down. So, I told her to lay down and rest. Later, that night, after Dad got home from visiting her, the Nursing Home called. They told him to get to the ER at the hospital as fast as he could. He got there immediately, and she passed away within just a few minutes of his arrival. I received a phone call from my uncle that morning around 5:00. He told me about mom and, of course, I said we were on our way to Illinois. Cary had not been well himself; he had an appointment with his specialist on the following Monday. We had Mom's visitation services on Friday night, and her funeral services on Saturday, the next day. We left for Georgia on Sunday so Cary could go to the doctor. I wanted to stay longer with my Dad, but he insisted that we go ahead and keep Cary's appointment. We arrived home very late that night. I kept Jordan out of school and he went to the doctor with us. The Doctor walked in and told us that my husband had cancer and had to be admitted to the hospital for surgery. The day after we drove back from my mother's funeral, we found out that Cary had cancer, and Jordan was with us. Jordan was only 10 years old. HUGE! So, I took a real deep breath, and asked God for all the help He could give me, because I knew I was going to need everything He had for me.

After several weeks of testing, we finally received a confirmed diagnosis. My precious husband was diagnosed with Stage 4 lung cancer with less than six months to live. Within two weeks, reality set in. It became very real to me what my responsibilities were. Cary was so weak he couldn't even drive. I made sure everything stayed as normal as possible for Jordan. He was in the gifted classes in the fifth grade. Of course, I notified everyone at school- his teacher, counselor, resource teacher, etc. They were very supportive. Jordan, however, wanted to stay home every day with his dad. But I was determined he would get his education. I would get Jordan ready for school every morning. Cary would get up about twenty minutes later. So, I would jump in the shower for twenty minutes. I could cry and pour out my heart to God and Cary could not hear me, because the water was running. Every day, I would ask my Heavenly Father, "God, You got any more of that stuff you gave me yesterday? "Cause I used it all up and I need some more". He would always bring the Scripture in II. Corinthians 12:9 to my mind. In this Scripture, the Lord reminds the apostle Paul that "my grace is sufficient for thee". That "stuff" He was supplying was called Grace.

Even though I was extremely busy, I still had time to reflect and ponder on some recent things that God had been revealing to me in my secret prayer life. I remember in February, 2005, God told me it was time for me to seek His wisdom. He was dealing very strongly with me about this. I already had my Bachelors of Science in Social Work, plus several other college courses. But God told me I had enough of man's wisdom and it was time I began to seek wisdom from above. So, I began to search the Scriptures for anything I could find on wisdom. I read the entire book of Proverbs, Ecclesiastes, and James. Little did I realize how much of God's wisdom I would need.

When we first received the initial diagnosis, Cary was an inpatient in the hospital in Athens, Georgia. The Oncologist (cancer) doctor came in and gave us the diagnosis of Stage 4 lung cancer. He went on to explain treatments and options. Then, he also told us it was time for us to "get our house in order". Cary and I both were just trying to get some sort of grip on the situation. Cary was 56. I was 46. The Doctor went ahead and left the room. I followed him out and I said, "Excuse me, sir". He turned around and said, "How can I help you?" I responded, "Can you tell me what I am dealing with here? I mean, how much longer...?" The Doctor said, "I can't tell you how much longer a man has to live." He started to walk away. I followed him and I said, "No, but based on your knowledge and expertise, you can tell me something. I mean, I have a 10-year old at home I have to think about." That is when he said, "less than six months". The Doctor walked away.

I went back to Cary's room and he was napping. I found the Chapel in the hospital as quickly as I could. I began to cry and once again, pour out my heart to my Heavenly Father. I didn't understand how or why this could be happening to us. I basically was questioning God. After all, Cary had recently become a Christian; we had a wonderful marriage; a very special son; and we were very much in love. We anticipated a very bright future; just living normal lives and serving our Lord and Master. My conversation with my Heavenly Father was quickly changing from a conversation to a whining session. I was like the proverbial sow, wallowing in a pile of muck, mire, and self-pity.

Finally, I quit complaining and got quiet long enough to give God time to speak to me. He dealt with me firmly and compassionately, at the same time. He reminded me that He is Sovereign. I will never forget the next things He spoke into my heart. He distinctly said "You _are_ my child. You _will_ hold up your head and smile, because you are _my daughter._ I love you with an everlasting love. So, go forth and let your light shine, so that you will be a witness for me. I love you with an undying love; for I will never leave thee or forsake thee". (Hebrews 13:5-6). So, I dried my tears, squared my shoulders back and walked out of the Chapel. I had the assurance in my heart that God was in control and He wasn't going anywhere. I also knew beyond the shadow of a doubt that He was working His will in our lives, even though it didn't hardly seem possible.

When the Dr. said it was time to get our affairs in order, that was the last thing on our minds. But, once again, God's provision of grace and wisdom were there. The first thing that had to be taken care of was Power of Attorney forms. I became Cary's Healthcare Power of Attorney and he filled out a Living Will. Then, we had to make out our legal wills. That was a difficult task. Then, we had to decide if Cary wanted a Do Not Resuscitate order. Then we had to decide on a legal guardian for Jordan, if something were to happen to me. Very difficult decisions. Not the type of decisions that you discuss at the dinner table. But we prayed over them, and once again, God's grace and wisdom were present, clearly in abundance. Then, I had to apply for SSDI benefits for Cary immediately since he could no longer work. I quit my job so I could take care of him. Usually, when you apply for SSDI, the process takes anywhere from several months to even years. However, our claim went through in ten days. The Social Security representative rushed it through because of the extreme circumstances. That was a blessing from God. In fact, we had more money when Cary was sick than we did when we were both working.

Thanksgiving and Christmas were rapidly approaching. I was doing everything in my power to keep life as normal as possible for Jordan. He continued to remain in school, against his wishes.

One particularly painful moment was when Cary had to be placed on home oxygen. Jordan came home on the bus and rushed in the house before I could stop him. He hurried to his dad to give him a hug, and saw that Cary was on oxygen. Jordan became so upset and asked me if his dad was going to die. That was the first time that I had to explain to him that his dad was very ill. I could no longer shelter him. I had to tell our son that his dad was fighting the ugly disease called cancer.

I told Jordan and held him as he cried. There was no one with me. No one except for my Heavenly Father, and He literally held me in His arms, while I held my son in mine. More grace, in abundance, being poured out.

Cary had an appointment with the doctor the day before Thanksgiving. My sister-in-law was watching Jordan for us. The Doctor said he could not give any more treatments to Cary; in fact, Cary's blood count was too low, and he needed two units to get his count built back up. After the appointment with the Dr., Cary said he wanted to go shopping. We went to a jewelry store. He gave me a kiss before we walked in and said, "Pick out what you want". Don't **ever** tell a lady to pick out what she wants in a jewelry store! I made out like a bandit. Cary got me a beautiful diamond necklace and earring set, and a beautiful three-stone diamond ring. We finished our Christmas shopping for Jordan, and then picked him up at Cary's sister's.

It was getting late when we got home. The plans for Thanksgiving were for Cary's family to gather at Cary's sister's home. She insisted that she would do most of the cooking, and that others could bring something in. She did not want me to worry about cooking anything for our family meal. I was so relieved that night when I finally got home. I was so tired; the last thing I wanted to do was cook or bake. But, Cary and Jordan's favorite pie was pumpkin.

At nine o'clock that night, Cary asked me to make him a pumpkin pie. I always had to make two pies, because Jordan would eat a whole pie by himself. I was so worn out, I could barely walk to the kitchen. But, I made two pumpkin pies. Cary had a piece of pie, just warm from the oven. He took one bite and said, "This really tastes good!" He had not even been able to drink one can of Ensure nutritional drink in an entire day, yet he ate a piece of warm pumpkin pie in one sitting. That was the last time he was able to eat anything at all. I will never regret making those pumpkin pies. Precious memories.

The following Monday afternoon, my Dad came down from Illinois to be with us. Later, the same afternoon, Cary was admitted to the hospital. He never made it back home. I stayed at the hospital with him. My dad took care of Jordan for me. Ten days later, Cary went home to be with Jesus. We had memorial services for him on Friday night in Georgia, and the next morning, we packed everything and moved up to Illinois to be with Dad. The following Monday, we had his funeral services.

Part 3

When a woman has been traumatized, she has been through a life-changing event. An event like what she has experienced requires every bit of strength she can muster to get out of bed. That is where God's Amazing Grace walks in and covers the situation. II Corinthians 12:9, the Apostle Paul says,

*"And He said unto me, 'My grace is sufficient for thee: for my strength is made perfect in weakness.'...*The Apostle Paul continues to say, *"Most gladly therefore will I rather glory in my infirmities, that the power of Christ may rest upon me."* The apostle Paul had sought the Lord three times over something he referred to as a "thorn in his flesh", that God would take it away from him, or remove it. Instead of getting the answer he thought he would get, the apostle Paul received the promise of the abundance of God's grace and that His grace would be sufficient. Yes, His grace is sufficient. It is more than enough. In every situation that is mentioned in this chapter, I had to ask God for more grace. He was faithful to answer my prayer. I found there was always plenty of grace to carry me through the different sufferings I had been through. The three people that were closest to me passed away. My sister, my Mother, and my husband. And there was always someone else who needed me to be strong for them. So, I took a deep breath. And I sighed. And I choked back my tears. Suffering in Silence. No one ever knew the heartache that I carried on the inside. No one but my Jesus. And I would cry in my pillow at night, because I would not be able to sleep. He would be right there to hear every cry, to wipe every tear. And I am no one special.

When you feel like you can't take another step; when you feel so weak, you may collapse at any moment; when you feel like you can't even take another breath, because the burden is so heavy, just ask our Savior to give you grace. He will always answer that prayer. You will feel your weakness crumble at His feet. You will feel yourself instantly gain strength through

His grace to stand. Just to stand. He will give you what you need for that very moment if you will ask Him. Remember, that is why it is called Amazing Grace by the old songwriter. Here are some of the words of that famous song:

Amazing Grace

"How sweet the sound,

That saved a wretch like me!

I once was lost, but now am found,

Was blind, but now I see."

What A Friend

Loneliness. Lonely. Being alone. These words just echo with emptiness. Empty-a void-a hole. A hole that needs to be filled to be filled. But not filled with just anything. I am very selective about what fills my hole. Because, you see, my void is in my heart. And because of that void, I have empty arms. There's that word empty again.

You see, the hole in my heart was created several years ago. Over thirty years, to be exact. In 1982, the most precious child was born. She was a beautiful little girl. And she was placed in <u>my </u>arms. Yes, that beautiful child was mine. My baby girl. God's masterpiece. But, He blessed me with her. Oh, what a delight she was! A little piece of heaven for me to enjoy on earth. I loved her with every ounce of my being. Every fiber within me-down to the very depths of my soul. In 1985, another precious child was born. She was a beautiful little girl. And she was placed in <u>my </u>arms. Yes, that beautiful child was mine. My second baby girl. God's masterpiece. He blessed me with a second beauty. She, too, was a delight! Another piece of heaven for me to enjoy on earth. I loved her with every ounce of my being. Every fiber within me-down to the very depths of my soul.

In 1988, something terrible happened. I still don't totally understand what happened. But, for some reason, I got very sick. I mean very, very sick. I was unable to function in life. I was placed in a psychiatric hospital in St, Louis, Missouri. My marriage ended in divorce. I was forced to give up my children to the custody of their father. Yes, that is right. They were taken from me. Right out of my loving arms but never out of my heart. I went from a three-bedroom home full of children's laughter to a one-bedroom apartment filled with sadness and sorrow.

When a woman is abused or traumatized, one of the first things she experiences is loneliness. She has just been through one of the most horrific events in her life. She thinks that she is the only one that has ever been through anything so terrible. She feels so guilty and ashamed, she begins to isolate herself from her friends and family. She wonders how she was even able to survive such a terrible ordeal. She just knows that everyone will think that she is somehow less of a person because of what she has been through. And she is just certain everyone is blaming her for the awful incident.

She spends many hours alone trying to understand what happened. Why it happened. What she could have done to keep it from happening. She is totally alone with her thoughts. She may be surrounded by a roomful of people, but she feels like she is the only person on this planet earth. She feels like no one else understands what she has been through. All those crazy thoughts and feelings could only come from her mind. But instead of talking about them, she remains quiet. She doesn't want to give the impression that she may be losing her mind.

So, she doesn't talk about her feelings. She "Suffers in Silence". She feels so lonely, like she doesn't have a friend in the world. But that is where she is wrong. I grieved over my children in silence, thinking I was the only mother in those circumstances. It took me several years to realize I was not the only person that had suffered such a loss. Just to have your children torn out of your arms due to something that wasn't your fault. And I certainly was not the first woman in the world who had spent endless nights alone-all alone.

But I wasn't alone. Because you see, I had a Friend. He is still my best Friend. He will be your Friend, too. He will never leave your side, no matter what the situation. No matter how large the hole in your heart; no matter how big the void. He will be there. It doesn't make any difference how long the dark, lonely nights are. He has a Book full of promises, called the Bible. One of the promises is found in the book of Hebrews, the 13th chapter, verses 5-6:

v.5 *"...for I will never leave thee, nor forsake thee.* (KJV)

There is another Scripture found in the book of St. Matthew 28:20:

v.20 '*...lo, I am with you always, even to the end of the world."*

So, you see, the Savior promises to always be with us, even to the end of the world. He doesn't want you to be alone and "Suffer in Silence". There is on old hymn that tells about what a true Friend we have when we allow Jesus to be our Friend. Here are some of the words:

What a Friend

"What a friend we have in Jesus,

All our sins and griefs to bear!

What a privilege to carry

Everything to God in prayer

O what peace we often forfeit...

O what needless pain we bear,

All because we do not carry...

Everything to God in prayer."

The Thieves

When a woman has been victimized or abused, she becomes prey to thieves. Perhaps not in the literal sense, but she is robbed, nonetheless. She may be robbed of her purity as a young girl. She may lose her dignity as a lady. She may lose some of her physical beauty due to the beatings she has had to endure and the scars that are left behind. But, she is also robbed of her self-esteem and her sense of self-worth. Her very basic survival needs may have been stolen. She may have been forced to leave her home, with nowhere to live. She may be without any finances to support herself. Her basic fear of feeling safe disappeared immediately. She has no where she can feel safe because of the terrible abuse she has endured. She feels as if she can trust no one. She is not sure she can even trust her own decision-making skills, judgement, wisdom, or anything else. She literally feels like she has lost all common sense and the ability to function in the world. Sometimes, things are so dark and bleak, she even loses the will to survive. But-she doesn't breathe a word to anyone. She would not want anyone to think she is going "crazy" or losing her mind. So, she keeps all those fears and irrational thoughts to herself, and she certainly doesn't share her story. She is "Suffering in Silence". But there is hope for the victim, even though she may not realize it. She feels totally hopeless, but the very opposite forces are on her side.

The thieves that robbed me of my treasures are no longer a part of my life anymore. God has worked another miracle. I am no longer a slave to the thieves. They had to bow down to the mighty name of Jesus. There is no other name greater than His. The thieves had to set me free. This same Jesus that set me free from the chains of bondage is the same One who made us the promise in John 10:10. He said,

"The thief cometh not but for to steal, and to kill, and destroy; I am come that they may have life, and they might have it more abundantly."

And he gives life. Now, they can no longer steal anything away from me, or my family. Jesus will destroy the thieves in your life as well. He is more than willing and able to help you through any attack of abuse that has created chaos and confusion in your life. Just trust in Him as your loving Savior. He will free you from any chains of bondage or thieves that have taken your life from you. He not only restores, He renews and refreshes; He replaces what has been stolen and lost with something so much better.

Mended Hearts

Broken hearts are a common language among women, especially those who have been traumatized or victimized. A victim's emotional state is very non-stable, and her heart has been broken, as well. The broken heart may be a result of grief over the death of a loved one. It may be broken because her marriage is in shambles. Maybe her family has been torn apart. Maybe she ran away from her from family. Maybe she was a victim of sexual assault. Perhaps she is facing a devastating disease. There are several reasons for a broken heart. Bottom line, her heart is broken.

When I went through the horrendous experience of having to give up custody of my two daughters, my heart felt like it shattered into a thousand pieces at my feet. I was in a tremendous amount of emotional pain. All I was able to do was cry. And weep. And cry some more. My eyes were continually filled with tears. My heart was filled with heaviness-too much heaviness. I continued to carry this burden. Every time I would see a small child or hear their laughter, my heart would crumble again.

I continued to carry and feel the pain, day after day. I looked for someone to care but couldn't find anyone. There were plenty of people to judge me, or to condemn me, but I couldn't find anyone to give comfort or consolation. I didn't even have permission to cry, because, somehow, the whole ugly mess was my fault. But the tears were like waterworks. When I was alone in the silence I cried. "Suffering in Silence".

There is a wonderful story in the Bible about a woman whose heart was broken. In the book of I Samuel, found in the Old Testament, we read an account of a lady named Hannah. She was married to a man named Elkanah. They worshipped and served God, according to the law. Hannah, however, could have no children. She was broken-hearted. She went to the temple and poured out her heart and soul to God. God gave her what she longed for. He blessed her with a son named Samuel. Hannah knew to turn to the God she served with her broken heart.

In my quiet moments, I, too would turn to God and His Word for comfort. In His Word, I find that He is always watching and listening to me. In Psalms 34:15, the Bible says,

"The eyes of the Lord are upon the righteous, and His ears are open to their cry." It is so refreshing to know that my Lord is watching over me and listening to my cries. Then, the psalmist goes on to say in verses 17-18,

Verse 17:*"The righteous cry and the Lord heareth, and delivereth them out of all of their troubles.*

Verse 18: *The Lord is nigh unto them that are of a broken heart; and saveth such as be of a contrite spirit".*

So, as I would cry out to God with my broken heart, His precious Holy Ghost would begin to work. The Spirit would begin ministering to my soul. He would begin to put together the shattered pieces of my heart. He would give comfort as only He can. Then, I would find myself in the arms of my Tender Shepherd-just resting-while my broken heart would begin to mend. Then, I would be reminded of this chorus,

I Know a Man Who Can

"I can't take a heart that's broken,

Make it over again,

But I know a Man who can…"

So, yes, my dear sister, you may feel as though your heart is broken, shattered in a thousand pieces. You may feel as though it will never be put back together again. But, just give all those broken pieces to the Savior. He will take each piece and lovingly put it back together. Even though you just knew you could never love as you once did, you will be able to love in a greater measure than you ever thought possible.

Post-Traumatic Stress Disorder: Part One

I often wondered who it was that thought of that name. Wonder if it was just some guy somewhere in a suit that had absolutely no idea what he was talking about. Someone that had no idea what it was like to experience it. Disorder makes it sound as trivial as a room that is cluttered and needs to be straightened up. Or a line that is supposed to be "straight" that isn't. But maybe he was on to something. Maybe that room was my mind. It certainly is cluttered and in disarray. All the boxes in my mind-my categories-have gotten blurred into a big mess. I used to be able to place different things in boxes in my mind. Issues that I was currently dealing with; issues that had been dealt with; and, issues that still required my attention. In boxes. Nice, neat boxes with labels. Everything placed in categories, all very organized. In a place where issues belong. All nicely and neatly labeled so I don't have to constantly open the box to find out what it contains.

Especially the issues I have already dealt with. The ones from my baby days. The ones from my childhood. The issues from when I was a young adult. The issues from my middle-age. An entire period of time called the past, which is just better off left forgotten. Because it is my past, I want to be able to block it out. Block it out. Erase it. Just forget it even exists. Keep only what I learned- only what I gleaned. Place it so far back in the corners of my mind that it can't escape.

You see, my past consists of ugly stuff. Bad memories that are so distasteful and rotten that they literally stink. Painful memories- so painful they make me cry all over again. As if I hadn't shed enough tears the first time around. Hot, burning tears-blinding tears.

But something happened in my recent past- less than seven years ago. Something that should have never happened. A "traumatic" event. A tragic event. Something I never thought would happen, especially in my life. Especially in my family's life. But it happened. It only lasted fifteen minutes. Fifteen minutes of terror. Fifteen minutes of horror. Fifteen minutes of "trauma" that have permanently changed my life.

It had been coming for a while. But the event only lasted fifteen minutes. What a fifteen minutes! I was physically abused. Never mind the emotional and mental abuse that had been taking place earlier. Maybe there is something to this thing called PTSD.

POST- After
TRAUMATIC-Relating to pain or a wound
STRESS-Strain
DISORDER-Chaos
Wonder if that gentleman in the suit had a clue…

Post-Traumatic Stress Disorder Part Two

And it happened again. When I swore it wouldn't. I strived so hard- so hard- to get this ugly thing called PTSD under control. I another episode, anyway. Actually, I am being too kind! It is not just ugly! It is HORRENDOUS! It is DARK! It is PURE EVIL! It is TORMENT! It is VIOLENT! It is FEAR! It is WICKED! It is PUSHY! It is AUDACIOUS! It is a BULLY! It is an Intruder, a Smart- Alec, an Interrupter, Rude, and Certainly, NO FRIEND OF MINE!

Post-Traumatic Stress Disorder is a group of symptoms that occur after a person has been through a life-altering event. The event may be rape; sexual violence/abuse; physical violence/abuse, domestic violence/abuse; emotional abuse; an accident; etc. Women who are victims of abuse usually suffer from PTSD. Often, they do not report the event. They do not think anyone will believe them; they may be afraid of retaliation; or they may feel as though there is no one who really cares. So, they think it will go away. The visible marks of the abuse will fade. The bruises will turn colors and then go away. The swelling will go down. The scratches will form scabs and heal over. Yes, the physical marks will go away. The woman may no longer be suffering physically.

But she is suffering emotionally. "Suffering in Silence". Quietly dealing with the invisible scars left by the abuse: A heightened startle response; fear of loud noises; trembling hands; etc. She is so afraid of the dark, she leaves all the lights on at night. She double locks her doors. Then, she puts a large object in front of the door, so no one can enter. Then, she tries to go to sleep. After much tossing and turning, she drifts off to sleep.

But, then, she is awakened by a nightmare. She is re-living the entire event in her sleep. She tries to scream and cry out, but she can't. Then, she quickly rises in her bed, and looks around. No one is there. But she needs to get out of bed to be certain. Her legs are she shaking as she carefully walks through the house. But everything is just like it was when she went to bed. Absolutely nothing is disturbed. Except her feeling of sanity. So, she goes back to bed, only to re-live the nightmare episode all over again. Then, morning breaks and it is time to awaken. Time to face another day filled with PTSD and "Suffer in Silence". Daytime brings "flashbacks". Flashbacks of the event. They are caused by "triggers".

Anything can be a trigger. She may be standing in line at the grocery store. She senses that there is someone behind her. She feels their breath as they inhale and exhale. Everything inside of her says to run. To flee as quickly as possible. Just find and exit and GO! Her pulse is racing. It feels like it is pounding straight through her chest. "Just Go!" is all she can hear. But, she refuses to make a scene. So, she waits in line. She is shaking so hard she can't count her money. She can't remember what she is doing at the grocery store. But she waits her turn and waits. She doesn't dare breathe a word to anyone. It is all she can do to breathe at all. "Suffering in Silence". She manages to get her groceries and finally leave.

She returns to her apartment. She double locks the doors. She breathes a sigh of relief. SAFE! SAFE! In her own home. She breathes another sigh of relief. Safe—or is she? Maybe she needs to check-- just to be sure. Even though she knows everything is alright, her mind is reminding her to check – just to be certain. She goes slowly into the kitchen. She checks the kitchen cabinets. No one in there. She goes to the living room and checks the coat closet.

The sleeve on a coat moves. She jumps back. There can't be anyone hiding in that closet. But she checks again. There is no one. It was just the opening of the closet door. She breathes another sigh of relief.

Next, she goes to the bedroom. She carefully opens the bedroom door. She checks under the bed. There is no one under there. So far, so good. Now, the bedroom closet is next. She carefully opens the door. There are only her clothes hanging in there. She goes to the bathroom. She gingerly pulls back the shower curtain. The shower is empty. Everywhere in her apartment is safe. So, she goes to her favorite chair to curl up with a book.

She closes her eyes and lets out a sigh of relief. SAFE—SAFE in her own apartment. Safe in her safety zone. But is she? When she closes her eyes, she sees him again. She sees the hatred in his eyes. She re-lives the episode of physical abuse happening all over again. She can physically feel the pain in her body just as if it were happening at that very moment. She can't breathe. Tears well up in her eyes. She dries her eyes as she opens them. She experienced another flashback.

She sits quietly for a few minutes. She needs to regain her composure. Then, she reaches for her favorite Book. The Book of all Ages which is infallible. The living Word. The Word of God. Her Bible. She opens it to Psalms 61:1-2.

Psalms 61:1-2. "Hear my cry, O God; attend unto my prayer.

V.2.From the end of the earth I will cry unto thee,

When my heart is overwhelmed, lead me to the Rock

That is higher than I".

She then begins to sing the old hymn,

"Rock of Ages, cleft for me, let me hide myself in Thee…"

If you are experiencing any type of PTSD, don't **ever** let anyone minimize what you are going through. Stop "Suffering in Silence". Keep telling your story until you find someone who will take the time to listen. Someone who really cares. Someone who believes in you. Someone you can trust. If you let PTSD go untreated, the effects will be harmful to your body. The stress will drain you. It will have a negative effect on your physical body. You will most certainly have emotional problems. The symptoms are unique from other emotional problems. It is not the same as having a mental illness.

You may experience an increased startle response. Your anxiety level will be through the roof. You may have panic attacks. You may find yourself more irritable than usual. You may re-live the incident in your sleep-that is known as nightmares. You may re-live the incident during the day-that is known as flashbacks. You may experience hallucinations or see shadows. You may develop trust issues. You may feel like there is no one you can truly trust, not even yourself. You may become depressed. You may even give up on life and feel as though life is not worth the effort. Suicidal thoughts may occupy your mind. They may become so intrusive, that suicide is all you are able to think about. The thoughts may be so overwhelming, you may even develop a plan. A plan to end everything. A plan to bring an end to the suffering.

But don't lose hope. There are trained professionals such as Social Workers and Counselors who will listen. They will keep listening as long as necessary. They will put you in touch with the proper authorities. They will be your advocate. They will ensure that you get the help that you need. They will take you by the hand and walk with you as you travel your journey to recovery.

Yes, it is a journey. A journey that takes time. Healing will take place on this journey. This type of healing can only be done through faith in God. He loves you and does not want you to suffer. That is why He designed the plan of salvation. He gave His only Son, Jesus Christ, to die for the sins of the world.

Jesus wants to save your soul and cleanse you from your sins. He wants to be your Friend. If you bring all your pain and hurt to Him, He will begin to heal your wounded soul. He wants you to trust Him with every care and worry. He will love you and accept you unconditionally. That is because of the tremendous amount of love He has for you. You can turn to Him anytime, day or night. He is waiting to hear your cries.

Whom Shall I Fear?

Fear. Afraid. These two words mean basically the same thing. There is the fear of heights; or fear of closed-in places; or a fear of crowds, or phobias. Phobias can be very frightening and disrupt your life. There is another type of fear known as dread. This is where you are anticipating that something bad is going to happen in the future. This may be based on past experiences or something that has been created in the imagination. But there is even a different type of fear. A fear that grips your heart. Clutches it tight. Takes away your breath. Makes breathing a labored effort. Takes away the ability to make sense of anything. Takes away all common sense.

When I had to face fear up close and personal, it wasn't just up close and personal. The fear I had to face was all-consuming. You see, it was the type of fear that had me totally paralyzed. Afraid to move. Afraid to speak, because my voice would tremble. If someone looked me in the eye, I would immediately begin to start to cry.

You see, what happened was so life-threatening, that I knew if I talked about it, I would have to re-live it. I couldn't make rational decisions, because my decision-making skills were clouded by this thing called fear. My ability to face another day was stretched beyond measure. Because when fear took over, it began to reside in the front part of my mind. It actually took up residence-moved in, with luggage, and all. Its' intent was to stay in my mind. But it did not come alone. You see, fear has a best friend known as torment.

Fear has a take-over attitude. When I tried to think of other things, the fear was so huge, it blocked every other thought out. But there was an ulterior motive. All the other thoughts were being blocked out so that torment could take over. The torment was that at any moment, the horrible event would happen all over again.

There were other factors that played into the torment. There were circumstances surrounding the event that made it more traumatic than usual. Those circumstances gave torment more of an opportunity to taunt me and remind me that the horrible event could happen in a moments' notice. Torment reminded me that the next phone call could be a trigger.

Fear and torment caused me to constantly be on guard. I was constantly looking over my shoulder, just in case someone was following me. I kept trying to get rid of the fear and torment in my mind, but I was constantly afraid. Sleep had left me long ago; I didn't even get hungry. My stomach just stayed tied up in knots. In the meantime, fear and torment had turned my mind into a playground. My emotions were all over the map. I had forgotten what it felt like to laugh. All I wanted to do was cry at the drop of a hat. Fear had managed to take over every nook and cranny of my mind. It had almost destroyed my spirit. It had tried to steal my soul.

The reason I was struggling with fear and torment was because I had been physically abused. Yes, I am a victim of physical abuse. All victims of abuse such as rape, domestic violence, sexual abuse, physical abuse, battered women's syndrome, elder abuse, etc. live and deal with fear and torment at a completely different level than others.

The degree to which the fear and torment consume their lives can't be imagined, unless you have been a victim yourself. Too many times, the victim just does her best to deal with the fear and torment alone. She thinks she is not supposed to talk about it. She "Suffers in Silence".

I, too" Suffered in Silence". BUT- then, I remembered. I remembered the One. The One who conquered fear itself. His name is Jesus Christ. And I turned to Him. No, I ran to Him. I ran as fast as I could. Yes, I ran straight to His open arms. His loving open arms. He embraced me gently but firmly. Firmly because He wanted to assure me that He was not letting me go. I was safe. Secure. Secure in His love. Then He gently whispered,

"Fear thou not; for I am with thee; for I am thy God: I will strengthen thee; yea, I will help thee; yea, I will uphold thee with the right hand of my righteousness." Isaiah 41:10 (KJV).

Isaac Houghton wrote a wonderful song about fear. The title is "Whom Shall I Fear?", and the Chorus goes like this:

"I know Who goes before me, I know Who stands behind,

The God of angel armies is always by my side.

The one who reigns forever, He is a friend of mine,

The God of angel armies is always by my side."

So, yes, fear and torment can be absolutely overwhelming. But we must remember that Jesus Christ conquered fear itself in the Garden of Gethsemane. Then, He was crucified on the cross. He overcame death, hell and the grave. We have no reason to fear if we belong to Him. Jesus promised to give us peace if we belong to Him. Here is one of His promises found in John 14:27:

"Peace I leave with you, My peace I give unto you: Not as the world giveth give I unto you. Let not your heart be troubled, neither let it be afraid." (KJV).

Joyful Mornings

Depression can strike at any time. It is defined as a psychological disorder that is characterized by sadness, inactivity, difficulty in thinking and concentrating, and feelings of dejection. It is an emotional state characterized by apathy, hopelessness and emptiness. The person will often experience a loss of appetite and/or weight. They will often lose a desire in things they used to enjoy. They may become very quiet and withdrawn from their friends.

Depression is like an emotional cancer. When cancer strikes the physical body, it often manifests with few symptoms in the early stages. And so it is with depression. Oftentimes, you will not realize you are depressed until the depression is very severe. In the same way that cancer destroys the physical body until there is absolutely nothing left, so it is with depression and the emotional state. Depression wreaks havoc in every realm of emotions that a person has until there is almost absolutely nothing left. They will often feel as if they can't feel anything anymore. Just like a cancer patient who is sedated on morphine for pain control. They cannot feel anything. They are numb to their physical pain. A person who is suffering from depression is numb to their emotions. They cannot feel their emotions because they are too painful. Depression leaves a person feeling hopeless and helpless. They feel as though every situation is beyond help and totally out of control.

When a woman has suffered abuse, it is very likely she will suffer from depression. She has been violated and traumatized. She may have been raped, sexually molested, a victim of domestic violence, or attempted murder. Maybe someone has broken into her home. Maybe she has been physically attacked. The key word is that she is a victim. She has been assaulted in one form or another. She tries to talk to different people, but no one will listen.

At first she doesn't experience the depression because she is in a state of shock. Then, suddenly, she feels herself slip into a hole. A deep hole.

Depression-My Mental Journey

I have been in that hole myself. I cried out for help, but no one was listening. Time went on, and I continued to"Suffer in Silence". Then, I began to slide deeper and deeper into that deep, dark hole. It was so deep it became a pit. The pit of despair. Each day, I continued to sink deeper. I was so low in the pit I could not see any light.

I cried and cried. I continued to cry. I cried until I had no more tears to shed. And I still cried. Crying inside. I shed tears that were invisible to anyone. Anyone that is, except the Heavenly Father. Crying out from within that only He can hear. I was feeling so hopeless that I knew there was no need to take one more step. I questioned if anyone really cared, and all the time, I knew they really didn't. I kept wondering if there was anything worthwhile outside of this deep, dark black hole of emptiness.

But, yet there was this thing called LIFE that I had to face. Yes---LIFE. But I didn't want to live. I didn't want to face life. I wanted to die. I was thinking of a way to get out of facing life. Just a way out. It didn't matter how I did it- I just had to get out. I just had to get out—plain and simple—get out. I began to devise plots and plans on how to get out. I was ashamed of myself for feeling like this – but no one, absolutely no one, knows what it feels like inside to carry all this inside. I tried to tell people what was going on, and I could tell they weren't really listening—it was obvious they didn't care.

Others may have been trying to understand. It was too overwhelming. Too much stuff. If I couldn't handle all of it, how could I expect anyone else to? The only human contact I had was other people telling me their problems. Inside, I was screaming, "NO MORE!". But outwardly I would say, "Of course, I will pray." And, honestly, I was not sure I could even muster up one more, "Dear Heavenly Father".

But I did. In the midst of my broken, shattered state. One more time. One more whisper. I called on His name. And I felt His ever-so-gentle tug on my heart, as He quietly reminded me He was there. He caressed me in His arms. Quiet. Stillness. Silence. Peace. No more turmoil in my mind. His presence hovered in every place where my mind was wrecked with torment.

I felt grace begin the work of re-assuring me that I belonged to the Savior. No matter how low I felt in my spirit, His Spirit reminded me of His grace. I am His. I could rest in that assurance. He reminded me that He is my burden-bearer. His spotlight shines in every area of darkness where fear and worry had their grip. As I release my burdens, one by one, they become His. He takes our burdens for us. We are not designed to carry such a heavy load. I began to feel the peace of God in my soul. The peace that the world can't understand. The peace that the world can't explain, because the source of peace comes from knowing Jesus as my Lord and Savior.

These words from an old hymn come to mind:

Peace, peace, wonderful peace

Coming down from the Father above,

Sweep over my spirit forever, I pray

In fathomless billows of love.

W. G. Cooper

The tears were flowing again. And I wept. And I wept and I cried some more. Humbled by His presence. Overcome by His love. Overwhelmed by His grace. Thankful I am His child.

Depression is something everyone deals with at some point in their lives. It occurs almost immediately after a woman has been abused. She loses all feelings of self-worth. The only emotion she can express is sadness, and that is expressed through her tears. She feels as if her life is over; and it is, as she once knew it. For her, life will never be the same. Something has been stolen from her. Everything that she held near and dear has been taken away by an intruder. A stranger. She has every reason to feel depressed. She has every reason to question why. She has every reason to wonder if things will ever be normal again.

So many different thoughts are racing through her head, as she is just trying to cope with the realities of everyday life. She is suffering." Suffering in Silence." But there is one she can turn to. His name is Jesus. He does not want her to suffer with all this pain she is trying to carry. He wants to take all that pain and depression on His shoulders, and just show how much He truly does love her.

The psalmist David states in Psalms 30:5

"...weeping may endure for a night but joy cometh in the morning."

It is not necessary for anyone to"Suffer in Silence". The greatest source of help is a result of trusting in Jesus Christ. He will pull you up out of the pit of despair. He will give you hope- even when it seems all hope is gone. Just trust Jesus.

Only Trust Him

Anxiety is very common among women. It can make you very nervous. Sometimes you feel very jumpy or jittery. Anxiety can manifest itself in many ways. Oftentimes, you will feel uneasy in your mind about something that is going to take place. You will have a sense of dread over something that has already taken place, as well. Anxiety is a part of our bodies' own natural reaction to excessive stress. Sometimes, there will be physical manifestations such as shaking or a trembling voice. Some people even experience excessive perspiration and rapid heartbeat due to anxiety. Anxiety can be caused by getting too many things on your mind or by trying to do too many things at once.

When I have difficulty with anxiety, oftentimes I have managed to take on the role of "Superwoman" along the way. The next thing I know, I have overloaded my schedule. As a result, I am totally overwhelmed. I find myself confused and frustrated. That is when I realize I have allowed far too many things to get on my mind. The mind can't process everything at the same time.

However, a woman who has been a victim of abuse or trauma suffers from a different type of anxiety. She experiences the type of anxiety that comes with knowing something horrible and dreadful will occur. But she just doesn't know when. It could be in the very next moment. Or it could be tonight, or even next week. It is the same feeling that occurs when one is "waiting for the other shoe to drop". She anticipates and waits in fear because she has experienced some sort of assault on her physical body. More than likely she has been threatened. Those threats echo in her head on a continual basis. 24 hours a day. 7 days a week. She lives in constant fear that the next attack on her body could happen in the very next moment. The next time the perpetrator decides to lash out. The next time he decides to take his rage out on her. The next time he decides she has done something wrong. This fear is true, even in the lives of rape victims. Most rapists enjoy torturing their victims before brutalizing them. The victim is anticipating inside her mind how much longer the torture will last. She is wondering how much longer he will continue to torment her. She wishes he would just kill her and get the suffering over with. But she is "Suffering in Silence". Since the victim has been abused before, she can't allow herself to relive how ugly things are going could get.

You see, it doesn't matter what type of abuse she has been through in the past. She is a VICTIM. A victim of abuse. She is going through trauma. Not only physical trauma to her body, but emotional trauma inside her mind. She may be screaming or begging for her life. Or, she may be silently weeping. Either way, she is experiencing a type of anxiety that only other victims can understand.

The Apostle Paul wrote some beautiful Scriptures in the book of Philippians that have been very helpful to me. These Scriptures reminded me of what I was supposed to think about when I was overcome with the anxiety that plagued me. They are found in Philippians 4:6-8. *v.6: be anxious for nothing, but in everything by prayer and supplication, with thanksgiving, let your requests be made known to God".*

V.7 and the peace of God, which passeth all understanding, shall keep your hearts and minds through Christ Jesus."

When we look at these two verses closely, we first see that Paul begins with the command to *"be anxious for nothing"*. The phrase means literally not to get anxious about anything. He continues to tell us how to bring our requests before God in verse 6. We are supposed to come before God with thanksgiving in our hearts with our hearts. Verse 7 continues on to promise us protection for our hearts and minds with the peace of God.

v.8" Finally, brethren, whatsoever things are true, whatsoever things are honest, whatsoever things are just, whatsoever things are pure, whatsoever things are lovely, whatsoever things are of a good report, and if there be any virtue, and if there be any praise, think on these things." (KJV)

If you are a victim of abuse, you could be wondering how it is possible to change your thoughts. You must be wondering how anyone in the situation of having their life threatened can focus their thoughts on something else. That is where Jesus, the Savior can help you. He will give you peace in the midst of that horrific storm. God's love will literally take your mind away from the present situation and allow your thoughts and mind to think on those things listed in Philippians 4:6-8. Your mind can be totally blinded to what you are going through. God can protect your mind from the ugliness of the situation you are experiencing. He will replace those thoughts with thoughts of peace and assurance in knowing you belong to Him. All you have to do is call on His name, and He will place a shield around your mind and thoughts. Just trust in Him completely. He has everything under control, even though it seems like things are total chaos at that very moment. Just trust in Him totally and completely and know that He is right by your side. Here is an old hymn that has been helpful to me over the years:

Only Trust Him

Only trust Him, Only trust Him

Only trust Him now.

He will save you, He will save you, He will save you now.

It Is Well

Worry and anxiety are almost identical twins, but yet, they are two totally different things. Anxiety is a sense of dread or feeling that something bad is about to take place; or it causes nervousness and fears over events that have taken place in the past. Worry, however, is when you allow your mind to be consumed with thoughts about future or past events. When a person worries about something, they have allowed their mind to run in several different directions about the same topic.

The world is full of bad news. When I turn the television on to watch the evening news, I find myself wanting to turn it off immediately. So much hatred, turmoil, violence, and "bad" news. There just seems to be so much to be worried about. But, when I am experiencing flare ups from PTSD, the things that are happening in the news seem to be so trivial. In fact, most of the time, my life is in chaos. I find myself worrying over every detail of my life. I am wondering if I am in a safe environment because, for some reason, I do not feel safe. I am worrying about when another episode of violent behavior will cross my path. Not just from the perpetrator, but from anyone. I am worried about the identity of the person who is standing behind me. Can I trust them to be so close to me? How will I ever feel safe again in this world? These are just a few examples of the things I worry about when I am experiencing another PTSD episode.

A victim of abuse certainly is bombarded with worrisome thoughts. The thoughts occupy every corner of her mind. They overshadow all logical thoughts and reasoning. There is no room in her mind for anything else. If she is a victim of rape, she will certainly be worried about her own physical safety. She may be worried about her health. She may be worried about what her family and friends will think if she tells about the rape. She may be worried that no one will believe her. A victim of domestic violence may be worried about her living arrangements. If she has children, she may be worried about their welfare.

Thoughts like these run rampant through the victim's mind. And this is just the tip of the iceberg. And iceberg it is. Because these thoughts are the ones that come with a spine-tingling chill. They will make the hair stand up on the back of your neck. All victims of abuse have that one thing in common- they have those worrisome thoughts. It is so difficult to stop worrying after you have been abused. But then, when I reach the point where I am totally consumed with worry,

I remember what Jesus said in John 16:33. He said, "...in this world ye shall have tribulation: but be of good cheer; I have overcome the world." (KJV).

God does not want His children to worry about anything. Jesus uses nature as an example of that in Matthew 6:25-34.

V.25."*Therefore I say unto you, Take no thought for your life, what ye shall eat, or what ye shall drink; nor yet for your body, what ye shall put on. Is not the life more than meat and the body more than raiment?*

V.26. "*Behold, the fowls of the air: for they sow not, neither do they reap, nor gather into barns; yet your heavenly Father feedeth them. Are ye not much better than they?*"

V.27. *Which of you taking thought can add one cubit unto his stature?*

V.28. *And why take ye thought for raiment? Consider the lilies of the field, how they grow; they toil not, neither do they spin:*

V.29. "*And yet I say unto you, That even Solomon in all his glory was not arrayed like one of these.*

V.30. "*Wherefore if God so clothe the grass of the field and today is, and tomorrow is cast into the oven, shall He not much more clothe you, O ye of little faith?*

V.31. *Therefore take no thought, saying, What shall we eat? or What shall we drink, or Wherewithal shall we be clothed?*

V.32. *(For after all these things do the Gentiles seek:) for your heavenly Father knoweth that ye have need of all these things.)*

V.33. "*But seek ye first the kingdom of God, and His righteousness; and all these things shall be added unto you.*

V. 34. "*Take therefore no thought for the morrow: for the morrow shall take thought for the things of itself. Sufficient unto the day is the evil thereof.*"

In this passage of Scripture, Jesus teaches us not to worry about anything. We are not even to worry about what we are going to eat, drink, or wear. Our Heavenly Father will take care of all those things for us. Jesus uses the birds of the air and the flowers of the field to illustrate His point. If the birds have nests, and the lilies are clothed with beauty and splendor, how much more will our Heavenly Father supply our needs? We just simply have to trust Him. Even though it is very difficult to trust anyone after an episode of abuse, we can trust our Father to take care of us, because we are His children. When we learn to trust in Him, we can have true peace, in spite of what has taken place. If we have believed in Jesus as our personal Savior and have placed our trust in our Heavenly Father to meet all of our needs, then we can truly say "It is well".

It Is Well

When peace like a river attendeth my way, When sorrows like sea
billows roll, Whatever my lot, Thou hast taught me to say,

"It is well, it is well, with my soul.

"It is well, (it is well), with my soul (with my soul)

It is well (it is well), with my soul!

Learning to Lean

When a woman has been through an episode of abuse, within seconds, her whole life has been turned upside down. Nothing in her world is normal any more. Her world has been rocked to the very core. The foundation she has been standing on begins to shake. She has been thrown totally off-balance, and barely has the ability to stand.

Sometimes, she is unable to stand on her own. Sometimes, she becomes very dependent. She may literally have to depend upon outside agencies for help. If she has been "kicked out" of her home, or her home is no longer a safe environment, she will need housing assistance. She may need help in getting food for her family. She may need financial help. She may need coverage for health care in the future. She will need professional counseling services. She will need assistance from the law enforcement agencies. She will most certainly need support from her family and friends. She will need support from a local clergy for spiritual strength to help her through one of the darkest moments of her life.

Most importantly, the victim will have to "learn to lean". She will be having to lean on others for her basic survival needs. Oftentimes, this is very difficult for her. Instead of making her needs known, for whatever reasons, she will remain silent. She may be too embarrassed to ask for help; or, she may not know help is available. Maybe she just does not know where to begin to ask for help. So, she remains quiet. She does not breathe one word about her needs. She "Suffers in Silence". But there is no need for her to handle all her needs alone.

There are agencies available to help victims of abuse. They are more than willing to help. (At the end of this chapter, you will find a listing of agencies and contact information). When the "event" took place in my life, I had to "learn to lean" on law enforcement and the legal system to ensure my physical safety. I had to lean on my counselor and PA for even more support. But, even beyond that, I had to lean, even harder, on my Heavenly Father. Oh, I had been a Christian since I was eight years old. But the "event" caused me to re-evaluate my relationship with Him.

I realized that He was as close as He had ever been. I spent more time in His Word. I spent more time in prayer. I spent more time in His worship. I spent more time in fellowship with Him. My relationship with Him has grown deeper and deeper. I have finally realized the meaning of the words "learning to lean".

Learning to Lean

"Learning to Lean, Learning to Lean,

I'm learning to lean on Jesus.

Finding more power than I ever dreamed,

I'm learning to lean on Jesus"

King Solomon gave us some very wise words of wisdom in the book of Proverbs about "learning to lean". Proverbs 3:5.

v.5: *"Trust in the Lord with all thine heart; and lean not to thine own understanding.*
v.6: *In all thy ways acknowledge him and he shall direct thy paths."*

The following is a partial list of agencies and contact information that is available to help victims of abuse:

1. Safe Horizon: 1-800-621-HOPE
2. SAFE HOME: 1-933-262-2868
3. National Resource on Domestic Violence
   Hotline Numbers: 1-800-537-2238 ext.5; TTY- 1-800-553-2508
4. National Domestic Violence Hotline: 1-800-799-SAFE (7233); TTY- 1-800-787-3224
5. Rape, Abuse and Incest National Network -1-800-656-HOPE (4673)
6. National Organization for Victim Assistance -1-800-TRY-NOVA
7. Battered Women's Justice Project: 1-800-903-0111 ext. 1
8. National Suicide Prevention Hotline: 1-800-273-8255
9. EMERGENCY 911

The Miracle of Forgiveness 33 Years

When someone has been involved in a situation that requires forgiveness, that person has been offended by someone else. I have just recently experienced the miracle of forgiveness in my life. I had a personal experience with forgiveness in which I learned a valuable lesson. Over 33 years ago, I was involved in an extremely emotionally painful situation. I had been married several years and had two beautiful children. I was a full-time mommy, had a full-time job, and worked full-time in the church.

I became very ill. For a while, the doctors did not know what was wrong. I was so sick that I would become unconscious and pass out. The doctors didn't know what was wrong. I was having what was known as "pseudo seizures", or false epileptic seizures. I became so ill I had to be hospitalized. That was when we received the diagnosis.

I was suffering from Major Depressive Disorder and needed psychiatric care. I had no one to talk to. No one to understand. "Suffering in Silence". I was carrying so much deep-rooted emotional pain inside my heart and I didn't know how to deal with it. At the same time, it was obvious I was unable to care for myself, let alone two children. My marriage fell apart. My children went to live with their father. Only a mother can know what that type of pain feels like. Only a mother can understand how it would feel to have her two most precious gifts ripped from her arms. Only a mother can relate.

There was a large hole in my heart that could not be filled. Just watching other mothers with their children would just about bring me to tears. Watching my parents missing out on spending time with their grandchildren was almost unbearable. Watching my mother break down and cry at the mention of their names was almost all I could handle. But I found comfort in my Friend, Jesus. Sometimes, all I could do was cry. And cry. And cry some more-and I would run out of tears; yet, I would still cry. I still turned to Him and served Him faithfully. He was always there for me. Thirty-three years later, I was still angry. I was still bitter. I harbored that in my heart for all those years. Oh, yes, I went to church. I served my Lord in what-ever capacity. I worked with and for my Pastors to help any way I could in the church. I made sure everyone knew how long I had been saved. But when I talked about

45

my ugly past, I could hear the bitterness in my voice. I felt it in my heart. I knew it was still there. The Holy Ghost would convict me during the altar calls, but I would not respond. I didn't feel as though I had to. After all, I had been wounded. I had been hurt as a mother. I deserved to be bitter and angry. I had to give up my children, and what mother has to do that? WHOA!!!! God finally shook me up and woke me up. That was no more than an excuse!

I had been allowing myself to stay angry and bitter, because somehow, I felt like I was entitled. I felt like I had a right to harbor sin in my heart, because I could excuse it away. I finally confessed my sins before my Lord. He was so gracious to forgive me. Now, I can talk about the situation and I don't feel the bitterness or anger that was once there. I can approach my Lord with a clean heart. I have been forgiven of something I was hanging on to for thirty-three years.

If you have experienced any type of abuse, you may have feelings of anger and bitterness toward your abuser. You may be angry at some family members who do not believe your story. You may have feelings of anger toward friends who betray you. You may be angry at the judicial system; you may be angry at the world; and you may even be angry at God. These feelings of anger and bitterness may be totally justified in your mind. You may find all types of reasons and excuses to harbor them. But, our Savior requires that we forgive. We can find that in the model prayer, known as the Lord's Prayer. He wants us to turn the feelings of anger and bitterness over to Him. Then we will be able to forgive.

Here is a beautiful example of forgiving others. I was going through some of my papers and found a wonderful treasure. It was written by a survivor of the Holocaust. At the age of ten years, she and her twin sister were separated from her parents and two older sisters. She never saw her family again. She and her sister became a part of a group of twin children that were used in medical and genetic testing under the direction of a Nazi Doctor. This young girl became gravely ill at which point the Dr. told her she only had two weeks to live. At that point, she stated she had proved him wrong. She had survived.

She then went on to say that in 1993 she had met another Nazi Doctor named Hans Munch. (From this point on is a direct quote from her work).

"I DECIDED TO FORGIVE HIM IN MY NAME ALONE.

I DECIDED TO FORGIVE ALL THE NAZIS FOR WHAT THEY DID TO ME. IT DIDN'T MEAN I WOULD FORGET THE PAST, OR THAT I WAS CONDONING WHAT THEY DID. IT MEANT THAT I WAS FINALLY FREE FROM THE BAGGAGE OF VICTIMHOOD.

I ENCOURAGE ALL VICTIMS OF TRAUMA AND VIOLENCE TO CONSIDER THE IDEA OF FORGIVENESS – NOT BECAUSE THE PERPETRATORS DESERVE IT, BUT BECAUSE THE VICTIMS DESERVE IT."

EVA MOLES KOR TAKEN TO AUSCHWITZ AT AGE 10 FOR MEDICAL EXPERIMENTATION BY DR. JOSEF MENGELE Even though I may have difficulty forgiving myself, I know One who is ever faithful to forgive me. I John 1:9 assures me that He will forgive me if I confess my sins. I have that guarantee. And so does everyone else. He wants to forgive you of your sins and cleanse you from all unrighteousness.

Epilogue

Immediately after the event, I went to work full-time at a local convenience store. I was also working part-time in the library at the local grade school. The PTSD symptoms were evident the very night the event took place. I did not know what was wrong, but I felt like I was barely surviving. I kept a lot of things to myself- I, too, allowed myself to" Suffer in Silence". I had to be hospitalized in a psychiatric facility. The first hospitalization occurred in October, 2011.

In April, of 2012, I had to have major surgery on my neck. At that time, my doctors recommended that I apply for Social Security Disability. I was not ready to stop working. I was only 55 years old. I followed their advice, however. I applied for Disability and was approved the first time.

When I went on Disability, I thought it was one of the worse things that could happen. I had to admit to myself and society that I was no longer able to work. But it has proven to be a true blessing. I have been able to spend more time with my Heavenly Father than ever before. As a victim of abuse and dealing with PTSD, this is the only way I have been able to survive. I have had several hospitalizations and continue to see a counselor. I am still in the care of Mr. Gabe Martin, PA-C., for medication management. My condition is much improved, however. It has been those quiet moments with my Heavenly Father that have made the difference. Many times, I have failed Him and stumbled. But never one time has He disappointed me.

Seven years later, my life is richer and fuller than it ever has been in many years. I have had the privilege of serving in my church under a wonderful pastor; I also have the honor of taking care of my elderly father, who just turned 90 years old this year. I am blessed with two beautiful granddaughters and one grandson. I am also beginning a new career as an author with plans to write children's books in the future. God continues to bless my life above and beyond anything I deserve. He continues to pour out His mercy and grace.

"Grace, grace, God's grace,

Grace that will pardon and cleanse within;

Grace, grace, God's grace,

Grace that is greater than all our sin."

My prayer is that this book has been a blessing to your heart. Hopefully, the Holy Spirit has been able to minister to your soul through these writings.

RCW

Biography

I am a 60-year old Christian lady from a small town in Southern Illinois. I lived in the state of Georgia for 13 years with my husband Cary, who is now deceased. After his passing, I moved back to Southern Illinois with our young son. I also have two daughters from a previous marriage; and three beautiful grandchildren. I was raised, along with my sister, in a strict Christian home. I am thankful every day for my parents. They were honest, God-fearing people that taught me to have a love for God and a very deep-seeded faith in Him and His Word. I have always had a love for reading. Many of my childhood hours were spent assisting the school librarian in elementary school. I always had a dream of someday writing a children's book, and actually having the book published.

As a woman, I have experienced several traumatic experiences. Through these experiences, I have had several years of counseling; while, at the same time, drawing closer to God thru His Word and prayer. These various experiences caused certain things, such as anxiety and depression. But there are Scriptures in God's Word which are helpful when dealing with these issues. God laid it on my heart to write an inspirational book designed exclusively to minister to the emotional needs of abused women.

To Him be all glory.

RCW

The author, Ms. Cox-White, would love to hear from her readers. If this book has helped you, please send e-mails to rlwsuperb@outlook.com

Printed in the United States
By Bookmasters